iPad on a Fast Track:

A Tutorial for iPad Beginners

Includes iOS 10

M. S. Stacy, Ph.D.
Anthony W. Varnon, DBA

First published in this edition 2016.

ISBN-13: 978-1539498704

Contents

INTRODUCTION

Fast Track describes the purpose and style of this book. You will begin using your new iPad as soon as you take it out of the box. With an economy of words and short hands-on exercises, you will be guided step by step through basic iPad procedures and the major applications.

By the book's end, you will be using the core Apple apps to find information on the internet, manage your email and messages, take photos and videos, listen to music, and make face-to-face calls with FaceTime. You will also be using applications such as Pages (a word processing app), Keynote (a presentation app) and Photon (a flash player for your iPad). Before you finish, you will have completed procedures to backup and protect your iPad and will know what to do if it is lost.

SET UP A NEW IPAD

To set up a new iPad, you must meet one of the following requirements:

- Be working in a Wi-Fi environment (the Wi-Fi symbol—two curved lines and a dot—is displayed at the upper left of the screen);

- OR have a cellular connection (the cellular provider is displayed at the upper left of the screen);

- OR have your iPad attached to a computer that has iTunes open (itunes.com).

    Hands-on: Complete each of the following steps to set up your new iPad.

1. Locate the Sleep/Wake button--the only button on the top right of the iPad when it is in portrait (upright) orientation.

2. Click the Sleep/Wake button to display the *Hello* screen.

    If the *Hello* screen is not shown after you click the Sleep/Wake button, you need to turn on the iPad power: **Press and hold** the Sleep/Wake button until an apple appears on the screen. Follow screen directions: >*slide to unlock* (slide the screen from left to right).

3. If the Hello screen asks you to *Press Home to open,* click the Home button, the only button at the bottom center of the screen.

4. Beginning with *Hello*, the iPad presents a series of screens requiring your action. While screens vary slightly between iPad Models, the following Setup Guide lists the basic setup screens and your responses.

- If the screen goes dark while you are working, click the Sleep/Wake button.
- If you need to start over with Setup, click the Home button to return to the *Hello* screen.

SETUP GUIDE FOR NEW IPAD

Screen	Your Response
Hello	Swipe (lightly press and drag) the screen from left to right
Language	Tap your language
Country or Region	Tap your country
Choose a Wi-Fi Network,	If you are working in Wi-Fi, tap your Wi-Fi network; type the Wi-Fi password, and tap *Join.* Otherwise, tap *Use Cellular Connection.*
Location Services	Tap *Enable Location Services*
Touch ID	Follow screen instructions to set up Touch ID, or tap Set Up Touch ID later.
Create a Passcode	If you want to use a passcode to lock your iPad, tap the code and then verify it by re-entering.
Apps & Data	Tap *Set Up as New IPad*

Apple ID	**If you already have an Apple ID**, tap the *Apple ID* example to bring up the keyboard. Type your ID and password. Then tap *Next,* upper right

If you do not have an Apple ID:
1. Tap *Don't have an Apple ID or forgot it?*
2. Tap *Create a Free Apple ID*
3. At the bottom of the Birthday screen, first scroll to your birthday **year** and then month/day (minimum age is 13). Tap *Next*
4. Type your name. Tap the keyboard *Return* key
5. Tap *Use Your current email address* OR tap *Create a free iCloud email address* (for example: JaneDoe@iCloud.com)
6. Type your email address (your new Apple ID); then tap the keyboard *Return* key
7. Following screen instructions, create and verify your Apple password; tap the keyboard *Return* key

Security Question 1 of 3 Security Question 2 of 3 Security Question 3 of 3	If you created a new Apple ID, you will be asked to set up three security questions and answers
Email Updates	Leave turned on (as is)
Terms and Conditions	Tap *Send by Email*
Send Terms Email	Type your email address; tap *Return* key.
iCloud Keychain	Tap *Don't Restore Passwords; Continue*
Siri	Tap *Turn On Siri*
Diagnostics	Tap *Send to Apple*
App Analytics	Tap *Share with App Developers*
Welcome to iPad	Tap *Get Started*

3

WORK WITH APPS

Meet the Home screen

Orientation. The Home screen can be displayed in either portrait (upright) or landscape (horizontal) orientation. To change the orientation while you are working, simply rotate the iPad.

Apple apps. The Home screen displays icons that open the apps on your iPad.

>*Hands-on: Locate the following apps on the Home screen:*
>***iTunes Store****, for purchasing music*
>***App Store****, for getting more apps*
>***Music****, for listening to music*

Extended app screen. The Home screen is not large enough to display all apps. Additional apps extend onto a second screen.

>*Hands-on: Swipe (press lightly and move) the screen from right to left to display an additional app screen.   Locate the Game Center app.*

The Dock. The area at the bottom of the screen is the Dock. The apps in the Dock are those you use most frequently; e.g., Safari (an internet app) and Mail. The apps in the Dock remain the same when you move between the app screens.

>*Hands-on: Swipe between the two app screens, noting the Dock apps.*

Open and close apps

Open an app. To open an app, tap the app icon on the Home screen.

>*Hands-on: Open the Clock app.* The timer is displayed; tap the other Clock options at the bottom of the screen.

Move back to the Home screen. When you are ready to leave an app and return to the Home screen, click the Home button: bottom center of the iPad in portrait orientation and side center in landscape orientation.   If you press the Home key too long, you will engage Siri, an app that responds to your voice requests. Click the Home button to turn Siri off.

Hands-on: Move from the Clock app back to the Home screen.

You can also move back to the Home screen by using a pinching gesture: press five fingers on the app screen, and rapidly pinch the fingers together.

Hands-on: Open the Safari app. Move back to the Home screen by pinching the screen. (Pinching may require a little practice!)

Close an app. Moving from an open app to the Home screen does not close the app; it remains open in the background. Closing an app begins with a double click of the Home button. Double click is a rapid click-click, not click and click.

Hands-on: Complete the following steps to close the Safari app.

1. Double click (click-click) the Home button.
2. Open apps appear in smaller screens. Swipe to the app you want to close.
3. Press and drag the app up and out of the window.
4. Click the Home button (or pinch five fingers) to return to the Home screen.

Add, delete, and move apps

Add a new app. The App Store offers millions of apps. As you add apps, the Home screen fills and expands into additional app windows.

Hands-on: Follow the steps below to add a free game to your iPad.

1. On the Home screen, tap the App Store icon.
2. Tap the Search box, upper right of the screen (includes a magnifying glass), to bring up the keyboard.
3. Type or dictate the kind of app you are looking for (e.g., free game). Or, if you know the name of the app, type or dictate its name in the Search box.
4. Tap the keyboard Search key.
5. Scroll through the suggested apps. If *Get* is displayed with an app, the app is free; otherwise, the price is shown. Tap *Get*.
6. Tap *Install*.

7. Type your case-sensitive Apple ID, and tap *OK*.
8. *Get* will be replaced by a circle that shows the progress of the download. When the download has completed, *Open* appears in place of the circle.
9. Tap *Open*.
10. To leave the app and return to the Home screen, click the Home button.
11. Locate the new app on the Home screen.

Hands-on: Search for the free Facebook app and install it. For additional practice, get these free apps: You Tube, iHeart Radio, Calculator Pro, WebMd, and BLB.

Delete unwanted apps. Apps that you have added can be deleted.

Hands-on: Follow the steps below to delete an app you have added.

1. On the Home screen, press the app icon until it starts to jiggle.
2. Tap the *x* on the icon, and then tap *Delete* in the pop-up window.
3. Turn off the *x's* on the other apps by clicking the Home button.

Move an app. You can rearrange your apps to fit your needs.

Hands-on: Move the App Store to the upper left of the Home screen and the Photos app from the second screen to the first.

1. On the Home screen, press the app icon until it starts jiggling.
2. Press and drag the app to the new location, and then release it.
3. Turn off the jiggling by clicking the Home button one time.

Apps can also be moved to, from, and within the Dock (maximum six apps). Decide which apps you will use most often and arrange the Dock to fit your needs.

USE OTHER BASICS

Recharge the iPad battery

The battery indicator, located at the upper right of the window, shows the percentage of battery charge remaining. When the charge is low, recharge the battery by using the USB cable and power connector provided with your iPad.

1. Insert the large end of the USB cable into the power connector.
2. Gently insert the small end of the USB cord into the cord slot on the bottom or side center of the iPad (depending on the orientation you are using).
3. Pull out the metal prongs on the power adaptor and connect the adaptor to a power outlet. When the charge reaches 100 percent, the charging will stop.

Update the operating system

Apple's new operating system iOS 10 was released in 2016 and its changes are included in this text. Check your operating system and update if necessary.

1. Open the Settings app from the Home Screen.
2. In the left panel, if *General* is not highlighted, tap it to highlight.
3. In the right panel, tap *Software Update*.
4. If you get the message *Your software is up to date*, close the Settings app by clicking the Home button.
5. To update your software, (a) be sure you are in a Wi-Fi environment, (b) connect your iPad to a power outlet, and (c) follow screen instructions to update your software. The update will take at least 30 minutes.

Control the sleep-wake time

Change the Auto-Lock setting. The iPad will go to sleep (go dark) after 2 minutes of non-use. To extend the awake time, change the Auto-Lock setting.

Hands-on: Follow these steps to change the Auto-Lock time to 15 minutes.

1. Open the *Settings* app from the Home screen.
2. In the left panel, tap *Display & Brightness* (or *General* if you have not updated to iOS 10).
3. In the right panel, tap *Auto-Lock*.
4. Tap the awake time of your choice (2 – 15 minutes or never go to sleep).
5. Click the Home button to return to the Home screen.

Use the Sleep/Wake button. To put the iPad to sleep immediately, click the Sleep/Wake button, top right in portrait orientation or upper left side in landscape orientation. Click the button again to re-awaken.

If you are using a protective case or cover that includes an automatic sleep/wake function, simply close or open the cover to put the iPad to sleep or awaken it.

Turn the power on and off

When the iPad will not be used for a longer period of time, turn the power off.

Very important: In addition to preserving the battery, turning the power off and on can be the solution when the iPad freezes or appears not to be working right.

Hands-on: Follow the steps below to turn the power off and then back on.

Turn the power off
1. Press the Sleep/Wake button until *>Slide to power off* is displayed.
2. Follow the screen instruction: *>Slide to power off.*

Turn the power on
1. Press the Sleep/Wake button until an apple appears. Wait.
2. Follow the screen instruction: *>slide to unlock.*
3. Enter your passcode.

Log on to a different Wi-Fi

When you use your iPad away from home, you will need to log on to different Wi-Fi's. Many public places offer Wi-Fi to those who know the password.

Check the Wi-Fi setting. To get your iPad ready to log on to different Wi-Fi's, confirm your iPad setting for joining networks.

Hands-on: Follow these steps to confirm or change your setting.

1. Open the Settings app from the Home screen.
2. In the left panel, tap *Wi-Fi.*
3. In the right panel, verify that *Ask to Join Networks* is turned on (if not, tap the button to turn it on).

Log on to a different Wi-Fi. The first time you use your iPad in a different Wi-Fi location, you will have to log on to the new Wi-Fi. When you return to that location, however, the iPad will automatically connect.

1. Open the Settings app from the Home screen.
2. In the left panel, tap *Wi-Fi*.
3. In the right panel, choose the desired Wi-Fi network. A network showing a lock requires a password.
4. Return to the Home screen by clicking the Home button.

Control volume and sounds

Use Volume buttons. The iPad has two Volume buttons. These buttons are located on the upper right side in portrait orientation or on the top left in landscape.
1. Click the first button to increase the volume.
2. Click the second button to decrease the volume.
3. Press (not click) the second button to mute the sound.

Set ringer and alerts volume. The Volume buttons can also control the volume of the ringer and alerts. However, if you want the ringer and alerts to be louder (or softer) than general audio, change the Sounds settings.
1. Open the Settings app from the Home screen.
2. In the left panel, tap *Sounds*.
3. In the right panel, slide the ball to increase or decrease the volume.
4. If *Change with Buttons* is turned on, tap the button to turn it off.
5. While you have the Sounds settings open, you may want to select the sounds you would like for the ringtone and various alerts.

Use the Side Switch to silence sounds. If your iPad has a Side Switch, it is a fast way to mute FaceTime calls, notifications, alerts, and sound effects. The Side Switch does not affect audio from music, videos, movies, or TV shows.

First, set up the Side Switch to be a mute button:
1. In the Settings app, tap *General* in the left panel.
2. In the right panel, under *Use Side Switch To*, tap *Mute*.

Use the Side Switch:
1. Locate the Side Switch: a tiny button next to the Volume buttons.

2. Turn the Side Switch on by pulling it toward the Volume buttons. An active switch reveals a red dot.
3. To turn the Side Switch off, push it away from the Volume buttons.

Use the Control Center to control sounds. The Control Center provides convenient access to iPad sound control.

Hands-on: Follow the steps below for an introduction to the role of the Control Center in controlling iPad sounds.

1. Open the Control Center by sweeping up from the bottom edge of the screen.
2. Locate the Media Controls: ◄◄ ► ►► (Previous, Play, and Forward) and a volume slide. To change the volume of music, videos, and other media, move the ball on the slide.
3. Locate the Moon, the icon for *Do Not Disturb*. To silence incoming FaceTime calls, notifications, and alerts—but not alarms or audio from music, videos, movies, or TV shows—tap the Moon. To turn off *Do Not Disturb,* tap the Moon again.

   To allow FaceTime calls when *Do Not Disturb* is on, change the settings:
   a. In the Settings left panel, tap *Do Not Disturb*.
   b. Tap *Allow Calls From*.
   c. *Tap Everyone, No One,* or *All Contacts*.
   d. While Settings is open, you may also want to change the *Silence* setting at the bottom of the panel to *Always* (locked or unlocked iPad).

4. In the center controls, your iPad may also have a Mute icon (microphone with line a through it). The Mute button works like the Side Switch to mute all sounds except audio from music or other media.
5. Close the Control Center by swiping down or by clicking the Home button.

Observe the Notifications Center

The Notifications Center provides information about your day—the date, the weather forecast, calendar events, alerts, and other notifications from various apps.
   1. Open the Notifications Center by swiping down from the top edge of any screen. (If your iPad is in a case, the top edge may be difficult to reach.)
   2. Close the Notifications Center by swiping up from the bottom of the screen.

Explore the iPad keyboards

When an app requires the use of a keyboard, the keyboard will either appear automatically in the bottom half of the window or you will tap an insert location on the screen to open the keyboard.

Hands-on: To bring up the keyboard for this introduction, open the Search window: Press the Home screen lightly and drag it down to display a Search box at the top of the window and a keyboard at the bottom of the window. Explore the keyboard, as outlined below.

Three keyboards. The iPad has three keyboards. To change between the keyboards, tap a keyboard button at the lower left of the window:

1. Numeric/Punctuation keyboard: Tap the *.?123* button.
2. Symbols keyboard: From the Numeric/Punctuation keyboard, tap the #+= button.
3. Alphabetic keyboard: Tap the *ABC* button.

Common features. Note the common features of all three keyboards:

1. The Backspace key at the end of the first row of keys.
2. A microphone preceding the Spacebar (for dictating your input).
3. An Emoji button preceding the microphone.
4. A Close Keyboard button at the lower right.

Click the Home key to return to the Home screen.

SET UP THE MAIL APP

The Mail app has to be set up to work with your email account. If you do not have the required information to set up your current account, you will be given the opportunity to create a free Google (Gmail) account in the steps below.

Hands-on: Follow all procedures in this section to set up the Mail app.

1. Open the Settings app.
2. In the left panel, scroll to *Mail.* Tap to select.

3. In the right panel, tap *Add Account.*
4. The right panel now includes a list of email providers and an *Other* option.

   If you see you see your email provider in the list, follow these steps:
   a. Tap the provider.
   b. Tap *Enter your email* to bring up the keyboard.
   c. Type your email address and tap *Next.*
   d. Tap the *Password* line; type your email password; tap *Next.*
   e. Tap *Save.*

   OR if your email provider is not listed:
   a. Tap *Other.*
   b. Complete the requested information. If you do not have the requested information, contact your email provider.

   OR set up a free Google (gmail) account now.
   a. In the provider list, tap *Google.*
   b. In the Gmail window, tap Mor*e options.*
   c. Tap *Create new account.*
   d. On the *Basic Information* page, enter your birth **year** first by tapping *Year* and then selecting the year. (If you are not at least 18 years old, you will not be able to complete the information). Then enter the remaining information by tapping the word (e.g., *Month, Day, Gender)* and then tapping a selection. Tap *Next.*
   e. Complete any remaining requested information.

5. Click the Home button to return to the Home screen.

CREATE YOUR CONTACTS

The Contacts app is the storage place for telephone numbers and email addresses needed for Mail, FaceTime, and Messages. Once stored, the addresses are automatically provided when they are needed.

Hands-on: Follow the steps below to create a few contacts.

1. Open the Contacts app from the Home screen.

2. The *Contacts* panel on the left will list the names of all contacts, while the panel on the right will provide the contact information.

3. Add a contact:
   a. Tap + at the top of the left panel.
   b. Enter the requested information. At the least, enter the first and last name, phone number, and email of each contact.
   c. Tap *Done*.

4. Edit a contact:
   a. With a contact open, tap *Edit* at the upper right of the window.
   b. Make any changes/additions.
   c. Tap *Done* to exit the Edit window.

5. Return to the Home screen by clicking the Home button.

   Hands-on: Edit one of your contacts.

USE THE MAIL APP

The Mail app is used to create, read, reply to, and forward email messages.

   Hands-on: For an introduction to the Mail app, complete each of the following procedures.

Create an email message

1. Open the Mail app from the Home screen.
2. Tap the Compose icon (pencil and pad) at the upper right.
3. Enter the addressee. If the name is in your Contacts, the address will appear in a list of possible names; tap the address. Otherwise, type the address.
4. Tap the *Subject* line, and type the subject.
5. Tap the message area, and type the message. Tap *Send*.
   OR, to save an email draft and finish it later, press the email title and drag it to the bottom of the screen. Tap the title to bring it back.

Insert a photo or video

1. Complete the email to the point you want to insert a photo or video.
2. Press the message area to bring up a menu.
3. Tap *Insert Photo or Video.*
4. Tap your selection and then tap *Use.*

Add an attachment to an email

1. Complete the email to the insertion point.
2. Press the message area to bring up a menu.
3. Tap *Add Attachment.*
4. Tap a selection. A link to the attachment will appear in the message area.

Dictate an email message

The microphone at the left of the keyboard Spacebar can be used to dictate email.

1. Tap the microphone. The wavy line across the bottom of the window indicates that the microphone is on. If the wavy line goes away, tap the microphone again.
2. Dictate and then tap *Done* to turn off the microphone.
3. Tap the window to correct any error.

Read an email

If you created a new Apple ID during your iPad setup, the letter from Apple with the subject "Verify your Apple ID" is important. Read that message and tap *Verify Now.* Then tap *Back to Mail* at the upper left of the window.

1. If *Inbox* (or *All Inboxes)* is not shown above the left panel, tap *<Mailboxes* and then *All Inboxes.*
2. Open an email by tapping the email sender in the left panel. The mail will open in the right panel.

Add a sender's email address to your Contacts

1. Tap the sender's name at the top of the email.
2. Select *Create New Contact* from the menu.
3. Complete the contact information.

Reply to or forward an email

1. Tap the left-pointing arrow at the upper right.
2. Tap *Reply* or *Forward*.
3. Complete the message and tap *Send.*

If the sender is one of your Contacts, you can reply with a different medium; for example, Message, FaceTime audio, or FaceTime video (covered in later sections).

1. Tap the sender's name at the top of the email.
2. From the bar beneath the sender's name, select a highlighted medium.

Search for an email

1. Drag the left panel down until a Search box shows at the top of the panel.
2. Tap the Search box, and begin entering a name or content word.
3. Tap a selection from the findings in the left panel.
4. To return to the Inbox, tap *Cancel* at the end of the Search box.

Delete email

1. To delete a single email:
   a. Tap the sender in the left panel.
   b. Tap the Trash icon at the upper right.
2. To delete multiple emails:
   a. In the left panel, tap *Edit.*
   b. For each email you want to delete, tap the button preceding the email.
   c. Tap *Trash* at the bottom of the panel.

USE SAFARI (THE INTERNET APP)

Safari is the internet app provided with the iPad. This section guides you through procedures for using this app to locate and use information from the internet.

Search the internet

Search for suggested sites.   You can use Safari to search for information about a specific topic; for example, persons, places, things, issues.

Hands-on: Open the Safari app and search for protective iPad cases.

1. Open the Safari app from the Home screen.

2. If you have previously used Safari, the last website you opened will be displayed. Tap the Search box at the top of the screen.

   The Search box is highlighted, and a panel of Favorites is displayed for quick retrieval. At this point, ignore the Favorites panel. You will later add your favorites to this panel.

3. You can tap the x at the end of the Search box to delete the current website, or just start typing your topic.   As soon as you begin entering, Safari suggests words and then topics based on your description. Select one of Safari's topics, or continue typing exactly what you want. When you have finished, tap the keyboard Go key.

   To dictate your search topic:
   a. Tap the Search box.
   b. Tap the microphone to the left of the keyboard Spacebar.
   c. Dictate your search topic, and tap *Done.*
   d. Tap the keyboard Go key.

4. A list of websites related to your topic will be displayed, including a line or two of text. Scroll the window up to view the suggested sites.

5. Open a site by tapping the blue text at the beginning of the entry.

6. To move back to the list of suggested topics:
   a. Locate the grey Tab Bar beneath the Search box. (You may have to press the window and pull down slightly to reveal the bar.) The Tab Bar includes a tab for each website that is open.
   b. The tab of the current website is highlighted. To move back to the list of suggested sites, tap the preceding tab.

Move directly to a specific website. When you know the address of a desired website, move directly to that site by entering the address in the Search box.

Hands-on: Search for nytimes.com, the website for the New York Times.

Search for a word or phrase on the website. With a website open, you can search for a specific word on the page.

Hands-on: Search for "health" on the New York Times page.

1. Locate the Share icon, an up arrow in a small box at the upper right.
2. Tap the Share icon.
3. In the bottom row of icons, scroll to *Find on Page*, and tap it.
4. The keyboard opens with a gray Find Bar directly above the keyboard. In the Search box of this bar, type a word or phrase; then tap the keyboard *Search* key.
5. The first occurrence of your word or phrase will be highlighted, and the Find Bar will move to the bottom of the window. The left end of the bar will include the number of occurrences found, as well as arrows to move between the occurrences. Tap an up or down arrow to see each occurrence.
6. Tap an occurrence to open, or tap *Done* at the end of the gray bar.

Return to a previous website

Use Previous and Next arrows. When highlighted, the Previous and Next arrows (< >) at the upper left of the Safari window move the screen to a previous or next website. Tap < to move to the previous website.

Use website tabs

1. Scroll the Tab Bar left or right to find the tab you want.

2. Tap the tab to move to the website.

Use the Browse window. The Browse icon (double box, upper right) opens a window showing all open websites.

1. Tap the Browse icon.
2. Active websites will be shown in miniature windows. Tap the desired site.

   Hands-on: Use the Browse window to reopen one of the iPad cases websites.

Use the History list. The History list includes websites you have visited in the last month. You can return to one of these websites by tapping it in the History list.

   Hands-on: Use the History panel to reopen the New York Times website.

1. To open the History panel, tap the *Bookmarks* icon (open book, upper left).
2. Tap *History* (if *History* is not displayed, tap *Bookmarks* to display it).
3. In the History list, tap the website you want to open.
4. Close the History panel by tapping the highlighted *Bookmarks* icon.

Refresh the website. After returning to a previous website, refresh it by tapping the Refresh icon (curved arrow) at the end of the Search box.

   Hands-on: Refresh the New York Times website. Then close the Bookmarks panel by tapping the now highlighted icon (to the left of the Search bar).

Close a website

Having an excessive number of open websites can cause Safari to slow down. Close the sites when you no longer need them.

Close the current website with the Tab Bar: Tap the x on the website tab.

Close several sites by using the Browse window

1. Tap the Browse icon (double-box, upper right).
2. Tap the x in the upper left corner of a website to close it.

3. Tap *Done* (upper right).

Hands-on: Close the current website from the Tab Bar and another website from the Browse window.

Reopen a recently-closed website

If you need a recently-closed website, you may still be able to retrieve it.

1. In the Safari window, press and hold the + at the upper right.
2. If the site is listed, tap it to reopen.

Hands-on: Reopen the New York Times website.

Close all open websites by erasing your History

1. Open the Settings app from the Home screen.
2. In the left panel, tap *Safari*.
3. Scroll the right panel down and tap *Clear History and Website Data*.
4. Tap *Clear*.

Use Reader View

Many websites have a Reader View that removes all advertising from the web page. If Reader View is available for the current website, the Reader View icon (a series of small lines) will be displayed at the left of the Search box.

Hands-on: Open the New York Times website (nytimes.com). Select Science in the topics bar. Then follow the instructions to remove the ads.

1. Tap the Reader View icon at the left of the Search box. (You may have to pull the window down to display the Search box.)
2. To return to the original window, tap the Reader View icon again.

Add a website to Favorites or the Reading List

You will often find a website that you want to use again. Two choices for saving the site for easy access are Favorites and Reading List.

Hands-on: Open the website discussions.apple.com/community/ipad and then complete the steps below to add it to your Favorites.

1. With the website open, tap the Share icon (upper right).
2. In the Share menu, bottom row, tap *Add to Favorites* or *Add to Reading List.*
3. Tap *Save.*

Retrieve from Favorites.   You can readily retrieve a Favorite by tapping it in the Favorites panel.

1. Open the Favorites panel by tapping the + at the upper right of the Safari window; tap the Favorite.
2. Or open the Favorites panel by tapping the Safari Search box; tap the Favorite.

Hands-on: Try each method to retrieve the iPad Communities site.

Retrieve from the Reading List

1. Tap the Bookmarks icon (open-book) at the upper left.
2. Tap the Reading Glass icon (eyeglasses).
3. Tap the website you want to use.
4. Close the Reading List panel by tapping the highlighted Bookmarks icon.

Hands-on: Add kahnacademy.com to your Reading List. Then retrieve.

Add a website to the Home screen

The *iPad User Guide* will be useful as you continue to use your iPad. By saving it to the Home screen, you will be able to open it just like any other app.

Hands-on: (a) Open the website support.apple.com. (b) In the Search box, enter "iPad User Guide." (c) Tap "iPad User Guide for iOS 10." (d) Complete the steps below to save the iPad User Guide to your Home screen.

1. Open the website you want to add to the Home screen.
2. Tap the Share icon, upper right.
3. In the Share menu, bottom row, tap *Add to Home Screen* and then *Add.*

Hands-on: Close the User Guide. Then re-open it from the Home screen.

Take a screen shot

When a website contains information you would like to keep, you can take a screen shot of the page. The screen shot will be saved in the Photos app.

1. Position your iPad screen exactly as you want to photograph it.
2. Press two buttons firmly and at the same time: the Sleep/Wake button and the Home button. Release. A white flash indicates the photo was taken.
3. On the Home screen, open the Photos app to view the screen shot.
4. Click the Home button to return to the Home screen.

Hands-on: Take a screen shot of your current screen. Then open the Photos app to see the shot.

Copy or save a website object

When a website includes a photo or other object you would like to keep, you may be able to save the object to the Photos app or copy it into another document.

Hands-on: Search for a drawing of the Eifel Tower, and save the drawing.

1. Press the object until *Save Image* and *Copy* appear. (Not all images will offer these choices.)
2. Tap *Save Image* to save it in the Photos app; or tap *Copy* and then paste the image into another document (press the document, and select *Paste*).
3. If you saved the object, open the Photos app to view your saved image.

Hands-on: View the photo in the Photos app.

Share a website

To share a website, send an email that contains a link to the website.

Hands-on: Send yourself a link to webmd.com.

1. With the website open in Safari, tap the Share icon.
2. In the Share menu, tap the Mail icon.
3. Note that the email message area now includes a link to the article (the website address). The recipient will tap the link to open the article.

Hands-on: Open the email and tap the link.

SEARCH WITH SIRI AND SPOTLIGHT

In addition to Safari, your iPad has two other search features, Siri and Spotlight.

Use Siri

With Siri you use your voice to communicate with the iPad. For example, you can ask Siri to search for information, check the weather, or open an app. Siri must be used in a Wi-Fi environment.

Select Siri's settings. First, select the voice you want Siri to use.

1. Open the Settings app from the Home screen.
2. In the left panel, tap *Siri.*
3. In the right panel, tap the *Siri* round button if it is not green.
4. Tap *Language* and select the language you want Siri to use.
5. Tap *<Siri* to move back to Siri settings
6. Tap *Siri Voice* and select *Accent* and *Gender* for Siri.
7. Click the Home button to return to the Home screen.

Use Siri to search

1. From any screen, engage Siri by pressing the Home button a few seconds.
2. A wavy line across the bottom of the screen indicates that Siri is listening. If Siri stops listening, the wavy line is replaced by a microphone. To re-engage Siri, tap the microphone. Speak the search information.
3. Tap a suggested site, or click the Home button to exit Siri.

Hands-on: Use Siri to search for medical websites.

Use Spotlight Search

Spotlight searches throughout your iPad--documents, notes, music, emails, internet--looking for information you request. Also, when your apps expand into several windows, Spotlight can help you move directly to a specific app.

You can access Spotlight from only the Home screen or its extended app screens.

1. Open Spotlight by pressing two fingers in the middle area of the screen (not the top edge), and pull down slightly.
2. Spotlight opens with Search box, as well as a list of frequently-used apps.
3. Tap the Search box, and enter your search information. Or tap an app to move directly to the app.
4. If you asked for information, select one of the displayed options, or click the Home button to return to the Home screen.

   Hands-on: Use Spotlight to search for "iPad help."

USE THE NOTES APP

The Notes app is a place to jot down important things you want to remember; for example, passwords and favorite quotes.

Get started with the Notes app

1. Open the Notes app from the Home screen.
2. Read the *Welcome* page, and then tap *Continue.*
3. Observe the two panels: The left panel lists the title and date of any current notes. The right panel contains the title and note content.
4. At the upper right, observe the icons: Delete, Share, Compose.

Create a note

   Hands-on: Create a note to make a record of your Wi-Fi password.

1. Begin a new note by tapping the Compose icon (pencil, upper right). The keyboard will open, and an insertion point will be blinking in the right panel.
2. To work with a full screen, tap the double arrows, upper left of the right panel.
3. Type (or tap the microphone and dictate) the title of your note.
4. Type (or dictate) the remainder of your note. If you dictate, tap *Done.*
5. If you were working in full screen, tap *<Notes* to exit full screen.

Change the style and content of a note

Hands-on: Begin a new note. Observe the gray tool bar directly above the keyboard; the icons on each end can be used to change the style and content of your note. Use each of the tool bar icons in the current note.

1. Undo, Redo, or Paste; when text is highlighted, this icon changes to Cut, Copy, Paste
2. Insert a Checklist; after completing a task, tap the circle to check off
3. Aa: Use a text style (Title, Heading, Body)
4. Aa: Create a list (Bullet, Dash, or Number)
5. Camera: Add a photo from your library, or take a photo or video
6. Write or create a drawing

Share a note

Hands-on: Share a note by Mail or Message.

1. Tap the Share icon, upper right.
2. Tap *Mail* or *Message.*

Find a note

Notes remain in the order in which they were created or last opened. If you prefer your notes listed alphabetically by title, change your Notes Settings to *Title.* To find a note quickly, use the Note Search box.

1. Scroll the left panel down until a Search box appears at the top of the panel.

2. Tap the Search box and enter your search word(s).
3. In the search results, tap any note you want to open.
4. To exit the search results, tap *Cancel* (right of the Search box).

Delete a note

With a note open, tap the Trash icon.

MULTITASK BETWEEN APPS

With multiple apps open, you can move between the apps as needed. For example, you may need to check the Calendar and Maps apps while you are reserving a flight or hotel on Safari.

> *Hands-on: Open the Calendar, Maps, and Safari apps. Try each method of moving between apps.*

Swipe between full-screen apps

If you have only a few apps open, this first method of multitasking is fast and easy.

1. With multiple apps open, press four fingers on the screen of one app.
2. Swipe left and/or right between the open apps.

Double-click the Home button

If several apps are open, this method lets you move quickly to a specific app.

1. Double-click (click-click) the Home button.
2. All open apps will appear in smaller screens. Scroll through the open apps by swiping the screens back and forth. Tap the app you want to work with.
3. If the app does not open full-screen, tap the screen again.

Use the Slide Over sidebar

This multi-tasking method opens a sidebar to display two apps in the same window.

1. Open the Slide Over sidebar by swiping in from the right edge of the screen.
2. An open app or a list of apps will be shown in the sidebar. To open a different app in the sidebar, press the top edge of the sidebar firmly and drag down to see a list of apps. (This step requires persistence!)
3. Tap the app you want open in the sidebar.
4. To close the sidebar, tap the app on the left.

USE COPY AND PASTE

Multitasking often involves copying something and pasting it somewhere else.

Copy and paste text

1. Press the beginning of the text to be copied and tap *Select*.
2. Arrange the beginning and ending dots to highlight all of the desired text, or tap *Select all* to copy the entire page.
3. Tap *Copy*.
4. Press the destination position to bring up a menu.
5. Tap *Paste*.

   Hands-on: Copy a paragraph from any website. Swipe to the Notes app, and paste the paragraph into a new note. Document the text by copying the web address from the website Search box and pasting it into the note.

Save and paste an object

1. Press the object to bring up a menu.
2. Tap *Save Image*.
3. Press the destination position and tap *Insert Photo*.
4. Tap your selection.
5. Tap *Use*.

Hands-on: Save an object from any website. Open Notes in the Slide Over sidebar. Paste the object and then its documentation into a new note.

USE THE CAMERA AND PHOTOS APPS

The Camera app is used to take both photos and videos. The photos and videos can be viewed in either the Camera app or the Photos app.

Hands-on: Throughout this camera section, complete each step for creating and working with photos and videos.

Take a photo

1. Open the Camera app from the Home screen or Control Center--or press the Home button and ask Siri to "open the Camera."
2. The screen displays the current camera view. If the Shutter button (the large round button) is white, the camera is ready to take a photo. If the button is red (for Video), tap *Photo* to change the button to white.
3. Get the view ready for the photo:
   a. To change the orientation of the photo, rotate the iPad.
   b. To reverse the view (i.e., take a self-photo), tap the Camera icon above the Shutter button.
   c. To zoom in or out, press two fingers on the screen and pinch out or in.
   d. To change the photo to square rather than rectangular, tap *Square*.
4. To take the photo, tap the white Shutter button.
5. To view the photo, tap the miniature photo next to the Shutter button.
6. To delete the photo, tap the Trash icon and then *Delete Photo*.
7. To return to the camera, tap *<Camera*, upper left.

Record a video

1. If the Shutter button is white (for Photo), tap *Video* to change to red.
2. To start recording, tap the red Shutter button. The button will change to a small red square, indicating that the video has begun.
3. Note that the time length of the video is displayed at the top of the screen.
4. To stop recording, tap the red square.

5. To view your video, tap the miniature photo adjacent to the Shutter button.
6. Tap the Play ▶ button.
7. At the end of the video, tap *<Camera.*

View photos and videos

Photos and videos can be viewed in either the Camera app or the Photos app. They can be viewed one at a time on a full screen or in groups according to dates and places they were taken.

1. In the Camera app, tap the miniature photo adjacent to the Shutter button to open the current photo/video.
2. To view the photos/videos one at a time, swipe left and right. A video is identified by the Play ▶ icon.
3. To view all photos/videos grouped by location and date, tap *All Photos.* The resulting window is the Moments view, showing the photos/videos in groups. In this view, videos are identified by a time length, lower right.
4. To open an individual item, tap the item.
5. To move from the item back to Moments, tap *<Moments* (upper left.

   Hands-on: Open the Photos app from the Home screen. Explore the contents of this app by tapping the various options.

Edit a photo

Editing tools are available to help you make changes in your photos.

   Hands-on: Use one of your photos to explore the editing tools.

1. Open a photo in full-screen view.
2. Tap the Edit icon (the icon to the right of the Trash icon*).*
3. The editing icons include the following:
   a. **Auto-enhance**: Tap to improve exposure and contrast.
   b. **Crop**: Tap to place borders around the photo, with tabs on each corner. Drag an outer border inward to cut the photo from one direction. Drag inward from a corner to cut the photo from two directions.
   c. **Photo filters**: Tap to apply different color effects.

    d. **Adjustments**: Set light, color, and black and white options.
    e. **Remove red eye**: Tap each eye that needs correcting.

4. Complete the edit and save by tapping *Done* (upper right).
5. To revert to the original, tap the photo; tap the Edit icon; tap Revert.

Share photos and videos

1. To share one photo or video: Tap in either the Camera or Photos app.

2. To share multiple photos/videos:
    a. Move to the screen containing the photos/videos.
    b. Tap *Select.*
    c. Tap each item.

3. To share all photos in a Moment:
    a. Move to the Moments screen.
    b. Tap *Select.*
    c. At the right end of the Moment, tap *Select.*
    d. Tap the Share icon.
    e. Tap a choice from the Share menu.

Delete photos and videos

1. Select the unwanted item(s).
2. Tap the Trash icon.

USE THE MESSAGES APP

With a Wi-Fi connection, you can use the Messages app to send free iMessages to other iPad, iPhone, iPod Touch, and Mac users. However, if either you or the other person is using a cellular network, data charges and other fees may apply.

Check settings for the Messages app

1. Open the Settings app from the Home screen.
2. In the left panel, select *Messages.*
3. In the right panel, confirm that *iMessage* is turned on. If not, tap the button.
4. In the right panel, tap *Send & Receive.*
5. In the right panel, confirm that your email address is checked.
6. At the top of the right panel, tap *<Messages.*
7. Review the remaining Messages settings by tapping the >:
   a. *Blocked:* locks out phone calls, messages, and FaceTime from specified persons in your Contacts. Tap *Add new* and select a contact to block.
   b. *Keep Messages:* Controls how long messages are kept.
   c. Check/change the remaining settings.
8. Return to the Home screen by clicking the Home button.

Hands-on: In the Settings app, confirm that iMessages is turned on in. Make choices in the remaining message settings.

Send a written message

1. Open the Messages app from the Home screen.
2. To begin a new message, tap the Compose icon in the left panel.
3. To select a recipient from your Contacts, tap the + at the end of the *To* box. Otherwise, type or dictate an email address or phone number. If the recipient shows up red, it is not registered with iMessage; delete by tapping the keyboard Backspace key twice.
4. To dictate any part of the message, tap the microphone to the left of the keyboard Spacebar.
5. Tap the *Subject* box, and enter the subject.
6. Tap the *iMessage* box (below the *Subject* box), and enter the message.
7. To send the message, tap the up arrow at the end of the message box.
8. Your message shows in a bubble in the right panel. Note that the *Subject* and message boxes are ready at the bottom of the screen for you to continue the conversation.
9. To start a new message to a different recipient, tap the Compose icon.
10. To open a different message, tap the message in the left panel.

Hands-on: Create and send a written message.

Send a voice message

Instead of a written message, you can record the message for a voice playback, using the recording microphone located at the end of the message box.

Hands-on: Follow the instructions below to create a voice message.

1. Enter the *To* line.
2. Ignore the *Subject* line in a voice message.
3. Press and hold the recording microphone (right end of the *iMessage* box) while you record your message. Then release the microphone.
4. To review the voice message, tap ▶ at the end of the message.
5. To accept and send the message, tap the up arrow (above the ▶).
   To cancel the message, tap the *x* at the beginning of the recording box.

Respond to a message

1. Tap the message in the left panel.
2. The *Subject* and *Messages* boxes for your response appear at the bottom of the right panel.

Include a photo or video in a message

Hands-on: Start a new message. Add a photo or video.

1. If an arrow appears before the *iMessage* box, tap it to display three icons.
2. Tap the Camera icon to bring up the Camera.
3. A panel fills the bottom portion of the window.
   a. The large photo is the current camera view. To use this view, tap the white Shutter button in the photo. To reverse the view, tap the Camera icon at the upper left of the large photo.
   b. The smaller photos at the right are recent photos. Tap to select.
   c. To select from other photos, tap *Photo Library;* tap a photo and *Use.*
   d. To take a photo or video for your message, tap the Camera icon. Tap *Done* to use the photo or video.
   e. To close the camera pane, tap the Camera icon at the left of the message box (you may have to tap > to display the Camera icon).

Include a handwritten message or a drawing

Hands-on: In a new message, add a handwritten message or drawing.

1. Tap the iMessage box, and note a new key on the bottom right of the keyboard. This is the Script key; tap it to open a pane in which you can write and/or draw.
2. Complete your writing or drawing; tap *Done* to add it to your message, or tap the Keyboard icon, lower right, to dismiss it.
3. Your handwritten message or drawing is automatically saved with other messages pre-created for your iPad. To use one of these iPad or personal messages or drawings:
   a. Begin your message by completing the *To* box.
   b. Tap the Apps icon immediately preceding the *iMessage* box (A in a bubble).
   c. Tap a message or drawing to move it into your document.
   d. To close the panel, tap the iMessage box or send the message.

Hands-on: In a new message, add a pre-created handwritten message.

Include music or images

1. Tap the Apps icon immediately preceding the iMessage box.
2. In the lower left corner, tap the four-dot icon.
3. Tap *Music* or *Images*.
4. Tap a selection.
5. Close the panel by tapping the *iMessage* box (or send the message).

Forward a message

1. Press the message bubble.
2. At the bottom of the screen, tap *More* and then the Forward icon.

Delete a message or conversation

1. Delete an individual message

a. In the right panel, press the message bubble.
b. At the bottom of the screen, tap *More*.
c. Tap the Trash icon and then *Delete Message*.

2. Delete a conversation
   a. In the left panel, press the message and drag it from right to left.
   b. Tap *Delete*.

Hands-on: Delete one of your message bubbles and a conversation.

USE THE FACETIME APP

FaceTime lets you talk face to face with others who have an iPad, iPhone, or iPod Touch. You can also use FaceTime to make a voice-only call.

Your iPad must be connected to the internet through Wi-Fi or a cellular connection. Using FaceTime with a cellular connection may result in additional charges, as well as use up a large amount of cellular data.

Confirm your FaceTime email address

The first step in using FaceTime is to establish where you can be reached.

Hands-on: Complete the steps below to confirm your FaceTime address.

1. Open the Settings app from the Home screen.
2. In the left panel, scroll to *FaceTime* and tap.
3. In the right panel, confirm that FaceTime is turned on.
4. Under *YOU CAN BE REACHED BY FACETIME AT,* make sure the email address associated with your iPad is listed and preceded by a checkmark. If it is not, tap "Add Another Email" and enter your email address. This email address will have to be verified before it can be used for FaceTime.
5. Click the Home button to return to the Home screen.

Begin a video FaceTime call

Hands-on: Begin a video FaceTime call by following these steps.

1. Open the FaceTime app.
2. Be sure *Video* (for face-to-face calls) is selected at the top of the left panel.
3. Identify the person you want to call:
   a. The left panel displays a list of recent callers. If the person you want to call is on this list, tap the name and the call will begin.
   b. For persons not in the recent-caller list, tap the + at the top of the left panel to display your Contacts. In the Contacts list, tap the name. Then tap the Camera icon to the right of the name. (If the Camera icon is dimmed, the person cannot receive a video call.)
   c. If the person is not listed in your Contacts, tap *Cancel* to leave the Contacts. Then type the email address, name, or phone number at the top of the left panel. Tap the Search key. If the Camera icon to the right of the name/address/phone number is highlighted, tap the icon; otherwise, tap *Cancel*.

Control the FaceTime volume

1. Use the two Volume buttons:
   a. Upper right side in portrait orientation.
   b. Top left in landscape orientation.

2. Or use the Control Center (swipe up from the bottom of the window)

Reverse the FaceTime camera

The FaceTime camera can be reversed to turn the view away from you.

1. With a call in progress, tap the bottom of the window to display a camera.
2. Tap the camera to reverse the view.
3. To change the view back, tap the camera again.

Use other apps during a FaceTime call

During a FaceTime call, you can open and use any other app—for example, you might want to check your email during your call. While the other app is open, FaceTime is still running.

1. During the FaceTime session, click the Home button to select an app.
2. Note that the app screen contains a path back to FaceTime: (a) a thin green line across the top of the window or (b) a miniature FaceTime window containing a Return icon in its lower left corner.
3. To move back to the FaceTime screen, tap the green line at the top of the window or the Return icon on the miniature FaceTime window.

End the FaceTime call

1. Tap the bottom of the FaceTime window to display a red phone.
2. Tap the red phone.

Make an audio FaceTime call

If you prefer not to be seen in a FaceTime call, make an audio call rather than a video call.

1. Open the FaceTime app.
2. Tap *Audio* at the top of the left panel.
3. Select the recipient.
4. Tap the Phone icon to the right of the name.

SET UP PAYMENT INFORMATION

The iPad has two stores from which you can make purchases: the App Store and the iTunes Store. To pay for app and music purchases, you must set up a payment method—an iTunes gift card, a credit card, or a debit card.

Redeem an iTunes gift card

iTunes gift cards can be used for purchases from both the App Store and the iTunes Store. The cards are available at a variety of places, including pharmacies and grocery stores. They can be redeemed online (deposited in your Apple account) from either of the iPad stores.

Hands-on: If you have an iTunes gift card, follow the steps below to redeem it now—or just follow the steps for an introduction to the procedure.

1. Redeem in the App Store:
   a. Open the App Store from the Home screen.
   b. If *Featured* is not showing at the top of the screen, tap *Featured* at the bottom of the screen.
2. OR, redeem in the iTunes Store:
   a. Open the iTunes Store from the Home screen.
   b. If *Music* is showing at the top of the screen, tap *Music* at the bottom of the screen.
3. Scroll to the bottom of screen and tap *Redeem.*
4. Enter your case-sensitive Apple password; tap *OK.*
5. At the bottom of the window, tap *You can also enter your code manually.*
6. Scratch off the code number on the gift card and enter the code.
7. Tap *Redeem* at the upper right.
8. Note that your Apple account balance is shown with your Apple ID at the lower left of the screen.

Set up a credit or debit card

Hands-on: If you are going to use a credit or debit card to pay for your app and/or music purchases, complete the following steps.

1. Open the Settings app from the Home screen.
2. In the left panel, scroll down and tap *iTunes & App Store.*
3. At the top of the right panel, tap your Apple ID.
4. Tap *View Apple ID.*

Note: If you get this screen message, *This Apple ID has not yet been used in the iTunes Store*, tap *Review.*

a. Tap your country and then *Next.*
   b. Tap *Send by Email.*
   c. Type your email address. Tap *Send.*
   d. To send the Terms and Conditions to your email, tap *OK.*
   e. Scroll to the bottom of the Terms and Conditions, and tap *Agree, Agree.*

5. Tap *Payment information.*
6. Tap your card type. Complete the remainder of the form.
7. Tap *Done.*
8. Click the Home button to return to the Home screen.

Send an iTunes gift card by email

If you have a debit or credit card as your method of payment, you can send an iTunes gift card to a friend (or to yourself) by email.

> *Hands-on: If you are going to use a credit or debit card to pay for your app and/or music purchases, complete the following steps.*

1. In the Featured window of the App Store (or the Music window of the iTunes Store), scroll to the bottom of the window and tap *Send Gift.*
2. Complete the *To, From,* and *Message* lines.
3. Tap the amount.
4. Tap the look of the gift card you want to send.
5. If you want to send the gift on a day other than today, change the date.
6. Tap *Next.*
7. Tap *Buy, BUY NOW, Buy,* and *Done.*
8. Click the Home button to return to the Home screen.

PURCHASE MUSIC FROM THE ITUNES STORE

Music can be purchased from the iTunes Store by (a) using iTunes gift credits you have added to your Apple account or (b) using a credit or debit card associated with your Apple account.

Find music to purchase

Hands-on: Follow the steps below to find music by a favorite artist.

1. Open the iTunes Store from the Home screen.
2. If Music is not showing at the top of window, tap *Music*, bottom left.
3. Tap the Search box (upper right).
4. Type the name of the artist, song, or album; then tap the keyboard *Search* key. (Or, dictate and tap *Done.)*

If you searched for an artist, the app will respond with a list of most popular songs by the artist, as well as a list of the artist's albums. If you searched for a particular song, the app will show all artists who recorded the song, as well as a list of albums containing the song.

Review a song before purchasing

1. Tap the song title or the album.
2. In the album list, tap the song title.
3. To stop playing the song, tap the song title again.

Hands-on: Begin listening to a song. Then stop the song.

Purchase an album or a song

1. Tap the $ amount for the album or the song.
2. Tap *Buy Album* or *Buy Song.*
3. Type your case-sensitive Apple password and then tap *OK.*

Automatically download purchases

If you use other devices (iPod, iPhone, computer) to purchase music, apps, or books, you will need to set up automatic downloads for your iPad.

Hands-on: Follow the steps below to set your iTunes and App Stores to automatically download purchases made on your other devices.

1. Open the Settings app from the Home screen.
2. In the left panel, tap *iTunes and App Store*.
3. In the right panel, *Automatic Downloads* should be turned on for each item in the list; if not, tap the circle to turn on.

Sync your iPad music with iTunes

If you have uploaded CDs to your computer iTunes account, you will need to sync your iPad Music app with your computer iTunes to download the CD songs.

> *Hands-on: Syncing your iPad with your computer iTunes may take more time than you want to spend at this time. If so, just review the steps.*

1. Open iTunes on your computer.
2. DO NOT connect your iPad to the computer.
3. Connect your iPad to a power source.
4. Be sure you are in a Wi-Fi environment (Wi-Fi symbol, upper left).
5. Open the Settings app from the Home screen.
6. In the left panel, tap *General*.
7. In the right panel, tap *iTunes Wi-Fi Sync*.
8. In the right panel, tap *Sync Now*.
9. When *Sync Now* lights up again, the sync is complete.

USE THE MUSIC APP

The Music app includes all of the songs you have purchased from the iTunes Store, It also includes any music you may have uploaded to your iTunes account on your computer and have subsequently synced with the iPad.

Select music for listening

1. Open the Music app from the Home screen. You may be encouraged to purchase Apple Music, a service that gives you access to millions of songs that you do not own. To remove the ad, tap *Not Now*.
2. Tap *Library,* upper left.
3. From the Library menu, select the way you want your music displayed.

4. Find the music you want to hear:
    a. To move directly to a specific artist, album, or song, enter the name in the Search box at the bottom of the screen.
    b. To move directly to selections beginning with a particular letter of the alphabet, locate the vertical alphabetic column and tap the letter.
5. Tap a selection to play.

Pause and resume the music

Music will continue playing until you tap the Pause button or close the Music app.

Hands-on: Start playing a song. Then practice the Pause and Resume buttons.

1. With a song playing, locate the two Media Control buttons at the lower right of the screen. The first is either Pause or Play, depending on whether music is currently playing. Tap Pause || to stop the music.
2. Tap Play ▶ to resume the music.
3. The other Media Control button ▶▶ will move the selection to the next song.

Change the music volume

In the Music app. While you are using the Music app, tap the currently playing song at the lower right to bring up the Media Controls.

From other apps. If, however, you are continuing to listen to music while you are reading email or performing other tasks on the iPad, use the Control Center to control the volume, as well as the other aspects of playing music (pausing, reversing, and forwarding). The Control Center is available from most app windows by swiping up from the bottom edge of the screen.

USE PAGES: THE WORD PROCESSING APP

Get started with Pages

Download the app. Pages is a word processing app created by Apple for the iPad.

1. Get the free *Pages* app from the App Store.
2. On the *Welcome to Pages* screen, tap *Continue.*
3. Tap *Use iCloud.*
4. Read the *Get Started* page.
5. Tap *Create a Document.*

Select a template. Documents in the Pages app begin with a template. You can use a blank template and do your own formatting, or you can use a template designed for a specific kind of document and modify it as needed.

1. On the Pages home screen, tap *Create Document* (first page in the window).
2. Scroll the *Choose a Template* screen up to see the available templates.
3. Tap the template that most closely meets your need.

   Hands-on: For your first document, select Essay from the Reports category.

Name your document. The template name appears at the top center of the page. As a first step, change this name to fit your document.

1. Tap the template name and enter your document name.
2. Tap the keyboard *Done* key.

   Hands-on: Change the name of your document to Essay Practice.

Use a designed template

Designed templates contain formatting and placeholder (sample) text. The basic procedure is to replace the placeholder text with your text.

Replace single-line placeholder text

1. Tap the placeholder text to highlight it. Don't delete the text because that would delete the formatting. If you delete in error, tap *Undo* (upper left).
2. Enter (type or dictate) your replacement text. Don't tap the Return key because that would add an unwanted blank line.

   Hands-on: Complete the introductory lines of the document (first five lines).

Replace placeholder paragraphs

1. Tap the placeholder paragraphs. Multiple paragraphs with the same format will be highlighted as one placeholder.
2. Replace the highlighted placeholder paragraphs by dictating (or typing) your replacement text.   Tap the Return key one time at the end of each paragraph.

   Hands-on: Enter two multi-line paragraphs.

Replace placeholder objects

1. Tap the + in the lower right corner of the object.
2. Select a replacement, or tap *Take Photo or Video.*

Manage documents

Save a document. To automatically save the document and return to the Pages home screen, tap *Documents,* upper left.

Open a saved document. Tap the miniature document on the Pages screen.

   Hands-on: Save your Practice Essay; then re-open it from Pages. Change the document name to Practice Essay 2. Save the document.

Delete a document

1. On the Pages screen, tap *Edit* (upper right).
2. Tap the document.
3. Tap the Trash icon, and *Delete Document.*

   Hands-on: Delete the Practice Essay 2 document.

Search for a document

1. Press the Pages screen and pull down to show the Search box.
2. Tap the Search box and enter the the word(s) you are looking for.
3. From the search results, tap a document to open, or tap *Cancel.*

Hands-on: Search for essay. Reopen Essay Practice.

Change text format

Whether you use a Blank template or a designed template, you can change text format before or after the text has been entered.

Use the Format menu

1. Place the flashing insertion point at the place the format change is to begin, or highlight text that has already been entered.
    a. To highlight one word, double-tap the word
    b. To highlight a line or paragraph, triple-tap
    c. To highlight a passage, double-tap the beginning; drag the dots.
    d. To highlight the entire document, press inside the text and tap *Select All.*
2. Tap the Format icon (paint brush, upper right).
3. Select one or more format changes: a Paragraph Style; a font type, size, and/or color; an effect (bold, italics, underscore, strikeout), text alignment, a list style, and/or line spacing.

    Hands-on: Make the following text format changes to the Essay Practice document: Opening three lines to right alignment; title color to black; any phrase to bold; add a bullet list of three items. As you work, don't forget the Undo button, upper left! Save your document.

Use the Shortcut Bar

The Shortcut Bar is the shaded row directly above the keyboard. The bar includes shortcuts for text formatting.

1. Tap →| to indent a single line or to *Indent* or *Outdent* paragraphs.
2. Tap *Helvetica* to change the font type.
3. Tap *AA* to change text size and text effects (bold, italics, underline).
4. Tap the Alignment icon to change text alignment: Left, center, right, justify.
5. Tap ¶ to insert a comment, page break, line break, column break, or footnote.

Hands-on: In your Essay Practice document, use the Shortcut Bar to change the opening three lines to left alignment, the text size of the paragraphs to 12, and the title to black bold. Underline a phrase.

Insert a footnote

1. Tap ¶ in the Shortcut Bar.
2. Tap *Footnote.*
3. The insertion point drops to the bottom of the page. Enter the footnote text.
4. Tap the text area above the footnote, and the insertion point will jump back up to the note number in the text.

Hands-on: Insert a footnote at the end of your first paragraph.

Add objects to the document

The Add Object icon + is used to add various objects to your document.

Add an object

Hands-on: Add a photo to your Essay Practice document.

1. Tap the Add Object icon, upper right.
2. Observe the kinds of objects: *Table, chart, text/shape, photo/video.*
3. Tap the icon of the object you want to add.
4. Blue dots around the border of the object show that the object is active. If there are no dots, press inside the object to activate the object.
5. Size the object: Drag the dots at the corners or sides. To size from two directions, drag a corner dot inward.
6. Move the object: With the object active, press and drag the object.
7. Make format changes: With the object active, tap the Format icon (paint brush) and select from the options.
8. Tap outside the object to deactivate.

Add a chart

Hands-on: Insert a pie chart into your document.

1. With the insertion point in position, tap the Add Object icon +.
2. Tap the Chart icon.
3. A sample chart appears in your document. Tap *Edit Data.*
4. In the Edit Data window, replace the sample data with your data.
5. In the Edit Data window, insert or delete columns and rows:
   a. Double-tap the shaded area preceding the column or row to highlight and bring up a menu.
   b. Select *Insert* or *Delete.*
   c. Tap *Done.*
6. Make format changes: With the chart active, tap the paint brush and select from the options.
7. Tap outside the chart to deactivate.

Delete an object: Tap the object; tap *Delete.*

Use the More menu

Explore the menu. Tap the More icon •••, upper right. Scroll through the menu to observe the contents.

Hands-on: Turn on Word Count in the Essay Practice document.

Insert a header and/or footer

1. In the More menu, tap *Document Setup.*
2. Tap the Header or Footer area, and enter text in any of the three areas.
3. Tap *Done.*

Hands-on: Add a page number header to your Essay Practice document.

Use Pages Help

Pages Help is a user guide available through the More menu.

1. In the More menu, tap *Pages Help.*
2. Tap the Menu icon (lines, upper left).
3. Scroll through the menu and tap a topic, or enter search information in the Search box.
4. When you are finished with Help, tap *Done.*

Hands-on: Add a table to your Essay Practice document. Use Pages Help as needed to complete the table.

USE KEYNOTE: THE PRESENTATION APP

Keynote, the Apple app for creating presentations, is free from the App Store.

Each presentation begins with the selection of a theme (an overall design). Each theme provides designed slides from which you choose as you build your presentation. The designed slides contain placeholder text and photos which you replace with your own text and photos. Keynote saves your file while you work.

Get started with Keynote

4. Get Keynote from the App Store.
5. At the Welcome screen, tap *Continue.*
6. Tap *Use iCloud* so that you can access your presentations from other devices.
7. Tap *My Presentations.*

Begin a presentation

1. In the Keynote window, tap *Create Presentation.*
2. Scroll the themes (basic designs); tap a selection.
3. Note that the left panel shows a miniature of your first slide, and the right panel is ready for you to develop the slide.
4. Tap the title shown at the top center, and enter (type or dictate) your title.

Hands-on: Select a theme, and change the presentation title. Tap Presentations (upper left) to return to the Keynote home page. Note that your file is shown directly following the Create Presentation page.

Replace placeholder text

Hands-on: Reopen your file, and replace the placeholder text with your text.

1. Double-tap placeholder text; type or dictate your replacement text.
2. To change the format of the replacement text:
   f. Tap the text and then the Format icon (paintbrush).
   g. Make any selections from the Style or Text menus.
   h. Click outside the menu to close.
3. To delete any unwanted text box, tap and select *Delete.*
4. To insert an additional text box, tap the Add Object icon +, upper right; select Shapes (the third object), and then *Text.* The box will expand as you enter text.
5. To move a text box, press and drag to the new location.

Add a slide

1. At the bottom of the left panel, tap +.
2. Tap a slide layout that most fits how you want the next slide to look.
3. Note that the slide has been added to the left panel and is displayed in the right panel.

   Hands-on: Add a slide that includes a photo.

Replace placeholder photos

1. Tap the x at the lower right of the photo.
2. Tap a replacement photo, or tap *Take Photo or Video.*

   Hands-on: Replace the placeholder photo with your photo.

Use a blank slide

Each presentation theme provides a blank slide that can be used to design a slide from scratch. It is especially useful when you want to include a table or chart.

Add text to a blank slide

1. Tap the Add Object icon +, upper right. Select *Text.*
2. Double-click the text box; type or dictate your text.

3. Press and drag the text box its desired location.
4. With the text box active, tap the Format icon (paint brush); format the text.

Hands-on: Select a blank slide. Use a text box to enter a title for your slide.

Add an object to a blank slide

1. Tap the Add Object icon +, upper right.
2. Tap the icon for table, chart, shape, or photo.
3. To size the object, drag the border dots.
4. To move the object, press and drag.
5. To format the object, tap the Format icon (paint brush); make any selections.

Hands-on: Add an object to your slide. It should be noted that the Add Object menu can be used to add objects and text boxes to any slide—not just blank slides.

Change the order of the slides

1. Press the miniature slide in the left panel.
2. Drag it up or down.

Add animation to a presentation

Animate text and objects

1. Tap the text or object, and select *Animate.*
2. Tap *None, Build in* or *None, Build out.*
3. Select an effect; then tap *Play* to preview.
4. If the slide has multiple animated items, select *Order* in the Animation menu; drag the items into the order you want them to come into view.
5. Review and consider the Options on the Animate *Options* menu.
6. Check your final animation by tapping *Play.*
7. Close the Animation window by tapping *Done*, upper right.

Hands-on: Animate text and an object on a slide.

Add a transition effect for the slide (how the slide comes into view)

1. In the right panel, press the slide to bring up a menu.
2. Tap *Transition,* and select a Transition Effect.
3. Tap *Play* to preview the transition.
4. Tap *Done,* upper right, to close the animation window

   Hands-on: Add a transition effect to the first slide.

Review the presentation

1. Tap the first slide in the panel on the left.
2. Tap the Play icon ▶, upper right.
3. Unless you changed the Options in the Animation menu, the presentation advances with a tap. Tap to advance each animation and each slide.
4. After reviewing the presentation, tap *Presentations* (upper left) to close the file.

   Hands-on: Add a few more slides to your presentation; then review your presentation. Return to the Presentations window when you are finished.

Use Keynote Help

1. With a presentation open, tap the More icon •••, upper right.
2. Tap *Keynote Help.*

   Hands-on: Use Keynote Help to get information on playing your presentation.

USE PHOTON FLASH PLAYER

Some internet sites require a flash player, usually mentioning Adobe Flash, which is not available for the iPad. A very good flash player at a reasonable price (about $5) is Photon Flash Player for iPads.

Hands-on: If you are ready to purchase Photon Flash, follow the steps below. Otherwise, the steps are here when you are ready.

1. Purchase *Photon Flash Player for iPads* from the App Store.
2. When a website indicates that a flash player is required, copy the website address (press the website address; tap *Select All,* and then *Copy).*
3. Open Photon Flash. Read *Flash Usage* and then tap *I Understand.*
4. Press the Photon Search box, select *Paste,* and tap the *Go* key.
5. Tap the lightning bolt (upper right) to start streaming.
6. If the lightning bolt reappears during your session, tap it again.

Hands-on: Open Socondigitalnetwork.com. Copy the website address and paste it into the Photon app. Select "See what's live now." Make a selection if one is available. Tap the lightning bolt to start streaming.

PROTECT YOUR IPAD

Several settings protect your documents and data, as well as the iPad itself.

Review iCloud Settings

1. Open the Settings app and select *iCloud.*
2. Tap each of the following settings and verify that it is turned on: *iCloud Drive, Backup, Keychain, Find My iPad,* and *Send Last Location.* Read the notes accompanying each setting. On the *Find My iPad* setting, follow the link *About Find My iPad and Privacy.*

Fraudulent Website Warning. In Safari settings, verify that *Fraudulent Website Warning* is activated. Be sure to follow the link *About Safari & Privacy.*

Use iCloud to find a missing iPad. If your iPad is missing in your home or if it was lost or stolen, use iCloud to find it.

1. On another device, go to www.icloud.com.
2. Select *Open Find My iPhone.*
3. Sign in with your Apple ID and password.
4. Select the device.
5. Open the Actions menu (bottom center).

6. Select one of the following:
   a. **Play Sound.** If you see from the map that your device is within hearing distance, select this option to locate the device.
   b. **Lost Mode.** This option will (1) lock the iPad with a passcode, (2) let you enter a custom message on the iPad screen (for example, how to reach you), and (3) keep track of the iPad's location.
   c. **Erase iPad.** This option will immediately erase your iPad if it is online; if not, the iPad will be erased when it is again online. If iCloud Backup was turned on before the iPad was erased, it can be restored from iCloud.

USE HELP SOURCES

iPad User Guide. In a previous section, you sent the *iPad User Guide* to the Home screen. This guide provides information on each Apple app.

Hands-on: Use the iPad User Guide to check out the Maps app.

The internet. Take your question to the internet with Safari or Spotlight Search.

Hands-on: Search for "How do I turn off iPhone calls on my iPad?"

Siri. Siri is always ready to help you find iPad information.

Hands-on: Ask Siri, "How can I organize my iPad apps into folders?"

Apple Support Communities. Consider joining an Apple Support Community, where you will have a group of iPad users with whom to share problems and solutions. In an earlier hands-on, you added this site to your Safari Favorites.

This FastTrack book. You will find the Table of Contents and the index of this book to be very helpful for review of various apps and procedures.

Thank you for selecting this book for your initial iPad journey!

INDEX